I CAN BE A

FIRE FIGHTER

By Rebecca Hankin

Prepared under the direction of Robert Hillerich, Ph.D.

CHILDRENS PRESS ™

CHICAGO

Library of Congress Cataloging in Publication Data

Hankin, Rebecca.
  I can be a fire fighter.
  (Includes index)
  Summary: Text and photographs introduce the important
work of fire fighters as they rescue people, fight fires,
give medical care, and make safety talks.
  1. Fire fighters—Juvenile literature. 2. Fire
extinction—Juvenile literature. [1. Fire fighters.
2. Occupations. 3. Fire extinction] I. Title.
TH9148.H35   1985   628.9'25   84-29282
ISBN 0-516-01847-7

PICTURE DICTIONARY

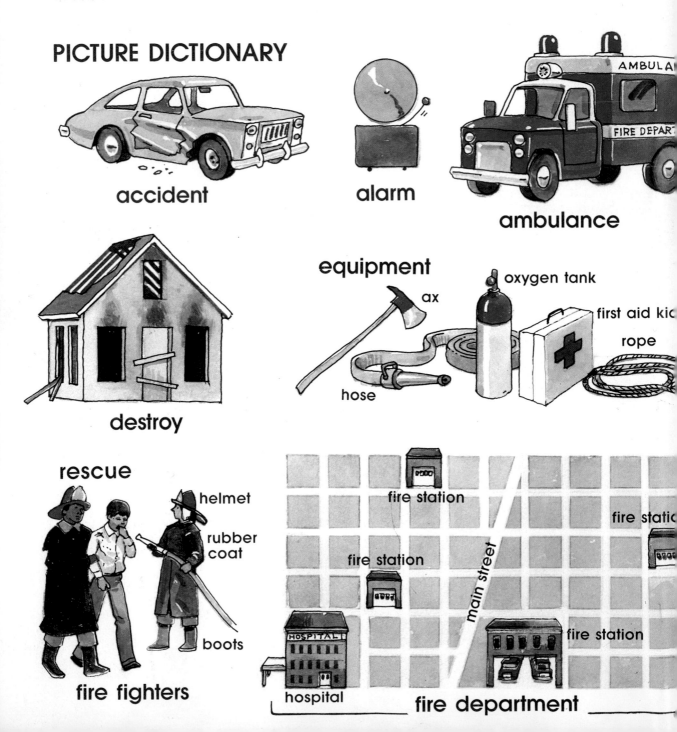

accident

alarm

ambulance

destroy

equipment

ax

oxygen tank

first aid kit

rope

hose

rescue

helmet

rubber coat

boots

fire fighters

fire station

fire station

fire station

fire station

main street

hospital

fire department

flood

inspect

medicine

paramedic

prevent

platform

ladder truck

pumper truck

stretcher

tornado

Fire is a dangerous thing. Each year fire destroys many homes and other buildings. People are hurt—sometimes killed—by fires.

Fire fighters are very important people. They work hard to save and protect all of us.

destroy

fire fighters

Radios are used to tell fire fighters where a fire is happening.

Many, many years ago there were no professional fire fighters. Often entire towns were destroyed by fires.

As the years passed, people learned how to work together to put out fires. Today, most towns and cities have fire departments.

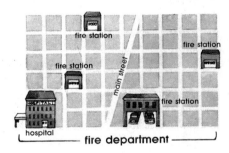

7

Fire fighters must learn
many things before they
can do their job well.
Many fire fighters go to a
special school.

rescue

They learn how to
rescue people. They
learn about fire trucks.
They learn how to put out
fires.

They learn how to give
medical care.
Fire fighters work hard
in school. They are
learning to save lives.

pumper truck

Most fire departments have two groups of fire fighters.

One group is called the engine company. These fire fighters work on trucks called pumpers.

Pumpers carry a pump and hoses that spray water on a fire.

The other group is called the ladder company. These fire

platform

ladder truck

fighters work on trucks
called ladder trucks.

Ladder trucks carry
large ladders and
platforms. The ladders
and platforms can be

raised into the air to
rescue people from
windows and other
high places.

Ladder trucks also
carry fire-fighting tools
and other rescue
equipment.

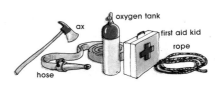

equipment

When an alarm sounds
in a fire station, both the
engine and ladder
companies race to the
fire. It takes them only a
few minutes to get there.

alarm

A fire officer tells fire
fighters from both groups
what to do.

The officer helps them
work together to put out
the fire.

Paramedics must have everything they will need before they go to a fire.

ambulance

paramedic

Fire department paramedics also rush to the scene of the fire. They give medical care to people who are hurt. Paramedics use ambulances to carry

important things like medicines, stretchers, and other equipment. If people must be taken to a hospital, paramedics drive them there in ambulances.

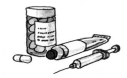
medicine

stretcher

hospital

Specially trained
fire fighters
find out how
a fire started.

After a fire is put out,
fire fighters try to find out
how it started. The fire
officer fills out a report
about the fire.

Fire fighters work hard
to put out fires and care
for people hurt by fires.
But they also work hard
to prevent fires before
they start.

prevent

Fire fighters teach
people about the
dangers of fire.
Sometimes they visit
schools to talk to students
about safety.

inspect

Some fire fighters
inspect homes, schools,

Fire drills are important at schools.

and places where
people work. If they see
something that is not
safe, fire fighters tell
people what needs to
be changed to make it
safe.

Fire fighters have other jobs, too.

When a tornado or flood strikes, they rescue people who need help.

Fire fighters also help people in accidents.

tornado

flood

accident

Fire fighters work hard
to help others. They put
out fires. They teach fire
safety rules. They help
people in tornadoes,
floods, and accidents.

A fire fighter's job is an
important one. Would you
like to be a fire fighter?

WORDS YOU SHOULD KNOW

accident (AK • sih • dent)—something that happens without planning and may hurt someone or damage something

ambulance (AM • byoo • lents)—a special car used to carry sick or hurt people

dangerous (DAINJ • er • uss)—likely to hurt someone or something

destroy (dih • STROY)—to ruin, wreck, or kill

equipment (ih • KWIP • ment)—things used to do something special. Fire hoses are equipment used to put out fires.

flood (FLUHD)—water that covers land that usually is dry

inspect (in • SPEKT)—to look at something very closely

medical (MED • ih • kil)—having to do with medicine and the care of people who are sick or hurt

paramedics (PAIR • uh • med • ix)—people trained to help others until they can be taken to a hospital

platform (PLAT • form)—a small, flat piece of floor that can be raised in the air

prevent (prih • VENT)—to keep something from happening

professional (pro • FESH • un • il)—doing something that requires skill or special training to earn money

protect (pro • TEKT)—to keep from being hurt or destroyed

pumpers (PUHM • perz)—fire trucks with pumps used to spray water on fires

report (ree • PORT)—a written, formal record about something that happened

rescue (RES • kyoo)—to save someone or something that is in danger

safety (SAYF • tee)—being safe; not being in danger of being hurt

tornado (tor • NAY • doh)—a very dangerous storm with strong winds that can destroy everything in its path

INDEX

PHOTO CREDITS

© Joseph Antos—4 (top), 15 (left)

© Bob Eckert/EKM-Nepenthe—37 (top)

©Tony Freeman—26 (bottom)

Hillstrom Stock Photo:

© John P. Faris—28 (bottom)
© Ray Hillstrom—14 (top right), 21, 22, 26 (top)
© Milt and Joan Mann—7, 12 (top right), 13, 16, 17 (left), 20, 24, 29 (right)
© Norma Morrison—25 (right)
© Mac Tavish—12 (top left)

Nawrocki Stock Photo:

© Candee Productions—15 (right)
© Ed Cordingley—19 (top)
© Joseph Jacobson/Journalism Services—Cover, 23 (right)
© Frank Neiman—17 (right)
© John Patsch/Journalism Services—Cover, 23 (right)
© Harry Prezekop—18, 19 (bottom)
© Steve Sumner/Journalism Services—4 (bottom), 14 (top left)

Courtesy Chicago Fire Department—6, 8 (2 photos), 9 (3 photos), 10 (2 photos),
11, 23 (left) 25 (left)

ABOUT THE AUTHOR

Rebecca Hankin is an author who lives and works in Chicago, Illinois.